JASVIR SINGH

The Gift of Family Time

A Calm and Comforting Guide for Busy Moms and Dads

First edition

ISBN: 979-8-9937593-6-4

This book was professionally typeset on Reedsy.
Find out more at reedsy.com

For my children,
and for my wife,
who shared the time that taught me what mattered,
and gave me the patience to notice it.

Contents

Introduction

You Don't Know It While It's Happening

I didn't know it was happening while it was happening.

That sounds obvious now. Almost foolish. But at the time, life just felt like it was moving. One day into the next. School drop-offs, work, dinner, homework, sleep. Repeat. Nothing dramatic. Nothing wrong. Just full days.

I thought family time was something clear. Something you'd recognize when it showed up. A vacation. A planned activity. A special day circled on the calendar. Something you could point to and say, *this counts.*

I didn't realize it was hiding in places I barely noticed.

It was in the car, when a question came from the back seat and I half-listened while thinking about what came next.

It was in the kitchen, when someone sat on the counter just to talk while I rushed through a task.

It was in the doorway at night, when a child lingered instead of going straight to bed.

Those moments didn't feel important. They felt ordinary. And ordinary things don't usually make us stop.

So I didn't.

For a long time, I believed family time was something I'd do more intentionally later. When work slowed down. When schedules settled. When life felt less demanding. When I wasn't always racing the clock.

Later felt reasonable. Responsible, even.

What I didn't understand was that later doesn't look back.

It keeps moving forward, whether we're ready or not.

I remember thinking that as long as we were together under the same roof, we were fine. That presence meant proximity. That being in the same space counted as connection.

But proximity is quiet.

It doesn't ask for attention.

A child can be in the same room as you and still be waiting for you.

Waiting for you to look up.

Waiting for you to respond without distraction.

Waiting for you to finish the sentence you started.

Those waits are small. Almost invisible. But they add up.

Some nights, family time looked like dinner at the table. Plates clinking. Someone talking about their day. Someone else barely listening. I remember nodding while scrolling, thinking I could multitask. That I was still there. That it didn't matter if my attention was split.

The conversation moved on without me.

I told myself it was fine. Kids talk. Kids repeat themselves. There would be more chances.

And there were.

Until there weren't.

There was a phase when questions came constantly.

Why is the sky that color?

Why do people argue?

Why do you have to work so much?

Can I tell you something?

The questions felt endless. Sometimes inconvenient. Sometimes exhausting. I remember wishing—more than once—for quiet.

I didn't realize then that questions are a form of closeness. A way of saying, *I trust you with my thoughts.*

No one tells you that the questions slow down.

They don't announce their exit. They just come less often. And then one day, you notice the quiet you once wanted is finally here.

And it doesn't feel the way you thought it would.

I don't remember the day it changed. That's the strange part. There was no clear line between then and now.

No argument.

No big transition.

No moment where someone said, "This is different."

I just noticed, one day, that conversations were shorter. Doors closed a little more often. Responses came quicker, thinner. The house felt quieter in a way I hadn't prepared for.

Not empty.

Just changed.

And suddenly, the moments I used to rush through felt heavy with meaning.

I found myself thinking about things I hadn't thought about in years. A child wanting to sit close for no reason. A story that went on too long. A small interruption I once found inconvenient.

I would have given anything to sit inside those moments again—just for a minute—with the awareness I have now.

Parents don't miss family time because they don't care.

They miss it because it doesn't ask to be protected.

Work demands attention loudly.

Deadlines insist.

Responsibilities announce themselves.

Family time doesn't.

It shows up quietly and assumes you'll notice. And when you don't, it doesn't argue. It just waits—until it can't.

I've thought a lot about why family time is so easy to overlook.

Part of it is busyness. Real busyness. The kind that comes from wanting to provide, to do right by your children, to keep everything running. That kind of busyness doesn't feel selfish. It feels responsible.

Another part is that family time doesn't look impressive from the outside.

No one applauds the ten minutes you sit on the floor listening to a rambling story.

No one celebrates the quiet car ride where nothing is said, but everything feels settled.

No one notices the evenings you choose not to rush a conversation.

Those moments don't post well. They don't measure well. They don't stand out.

But they last.

I'm not writing this as someone who did everything right.

I'm writing this as someone who recognized the value of certain moments only after they had already passed.

That isn't regret.

It's recognition.

Regret looks backward and freezes.

Recognition looks backward and understands.

And understanding changes how you move forward.

If you're reading this while your child is still in the next room, still asking questions, still finding reasons to be near you—even when they don't quite know why—then this book isn't about what you've missed.

It's about what you're living in right now.

You don't have to do anything drastic.

You don't have to reorganize your life.

You don't have to become a different parent.

You just have to notice what's already there.

Family time isn't measured in hours.

It's measured in availability.

In whether a child feels they can talk without being rushed.

In whether silence feels safe.

In whether being together feels easy, not earned.

Children don't remember how organized our lives were.

They remember how accessible we felt.

There were moments I thought didn't matter.

A child sitting on the stairs, waiting.

A conversation that started with, "This might be silly, but..."

A request that came at the worst possible time.

I answered some of them. I missed others.

At the time, I thought the missed ones would come back around.

They didn't.

They were replaced by independence. By privacy. By a natural turning outward that children are meant to do. Healthy. Necessary.

And still... hard.

I used to think confidence was built somewhere else. At school. Through achievement. Through experiences that looked impressive from the outside.

What I see now is that confidence begins much earlier. Much closer.

It begins in the way a child's voice is received at home.

In whether their thoughts are allowed to finish.

In whether their presence feels like a burden—or a welcome interruption.

Those things happen during family time.

Not the kind we plan.

The kind we overlook.

There's a moment many parents recognize, even if they don't talk about it much. The moment you realize your child doesn't need you in the same way anymore.

They still need you. Just differently.

That shift can feel confusing. Sometimes even like loss—though nothing is actually gone.

It's just moved.

That realization often brings everything before it into focus. The bedtime routines. The car conversations. The moments you were tired but showed up anyway.

You don't miss them because they were perfect.

You miss them because they were yours.

This book isn't a guide in the way most people think of guides.

There are no steps to follow.

No formulas to apply.

No checklist to complete.

It's a collection of moments, reflections, and realizations. Some small. Some uncomfortable. All honest.

It's about how family time changes as children grow.

How it slips away quietly.

And how much power it holds while it's still there.

You won't find perfect families in these pages.

You'll find busy ones. Tired ones. Loving ones who sometimes miss things—not because they don't care, but because they care about too many things at once.

You'll find moments that look ordinary on the surface and carry weight underneath.

If that sounds familiar, you're in the right place.

I wish someone had told me this earlier:

You don't lose family time all at once.

You lose it in pieces you don't think to save.

A conversation you postpone.

A moment you rush through.

A question you answer later instead of now.

None of them feel significant on their own.

Together, they become everything.

This book is about those pieces.

The ordinary ones.

The quiet ones.

The moments that don't feel important—until you realize they shaped everything.

It's about seeing them while they're still happening.

If you read this slowly, you might feel a small ache. That's normal.

Not guilt.

Just awareness.

Awareness of how much is happening right now that doesn't announce itself.

Awareness of how often the most meaningful parts of family life ask for almost nothing—except your attention.

If there's one thing to hold onto as you move forward, it's this:

Family time doesn't disappear because we don't value it.

It disappears because we don't realize when we're standing inside it.

And once you see it, you can't unsee it.

In the next chapter, we'll look at the moments that feel too small to matter—and why they matter more than almost anything else.

1

The Ordinary Moments We Don't Think to Save

There are moments we instinctively mark as important.

Birthdays. First days. Big wins. Big disappointments. We take pictures. We tell stories. We remember where we were standing.

And then there are the other moments.

The ones that don't feel like anything at all while they're happening.

Those are the ones that quietly shape everything.

Most days don't announce themselves.

They arrive already half-spent. Someone needs breakfast. Someone can't find a shoe. Someone is late. Someone is tired. The day moves before you've fully stepped into it.

Family time, in those moments, doesn't look like togetherness.

It looks like logistics.

And because it looks like logistics, we don't think to save it.

I remember evenings that felt like nothing.

Dinner that wasn't special.

Conversation that drifted.

A child talking while I washed dishes, half-listening, answering automatically.

At the time, I thought presence was about being in the same room.

I didn't realize presence had weight.

There's a kind of closeness that happens without ceremony.

It shows up when a child talks to you without planning what they're saying.

When they trail behind you from room to room.

When they start a sentence without knowing how it will end.

Those moments don't feel meaningful while they're happening.

They feel like background noise.

So we treat them like background noise.

Think about a regular car ride.

Not a long one. Not a road trip. Just the usual drive—school, practice, errands.

A question floats up from the back seat.

Something small. Something unpolished.

You answer it while watching traffic. Or you tell yourself you'll respond properly when you're not distracted. Or you say "uh-huh" and keep thinking about what's next.

Nothing dramatic happens.

The car keeps moving.

That moment passes.

You don't think to hold onto it.

What we don't realize is that these moments aren't waiting to become special.

They already are.

They just don't look like it.

There was a time when my children narrated their thoughts out loud.

Everything came with commentary.

Every idea wanted air.

Every observation needed to be shared immediately.

It felt endless.

Sometimes overwhelming.

Sometimes inconvenient.

I remember wishing—quietly—for fewer interruptions.

I didn't understand that interruption was the invitation.

Children don't wait for perfect timing.

They talk when they feel safe enough to talk.

That safety shows up in ordinary moments.

When you're folding laundry.

When you're brushing your teeth.

When you're doing something else entirely.

Those are the moments they choose.

Not the ones we schedule.

At the dinner table, I thought conversation would always be there.

Food on plates. Voices overlapping. Someone telling a story that went nowhere.

I thought it was background.

I thought it was constant.

I didn't realize it was fragile.

Ordinary moments feel unlimited.

That's the trick.

They feel like something we can return to whenever we want—later, tomorrow, next week.

We assume they repeat because they usually do.

Until one day, they don't.

There's a subtle shift that happens before we notice it.

A child answers instead of explains.

A story gets shorter.

A pause appears where conversation used to fill the space.

It doesn't feel like loss at first.

It feels like maturity.

Growth.

Independence.

And it is.

But it's also something else.

I used to believe that the moments that mattered most would stand out.

That I'd feel them when they happened.

That they'd announce themselves with emotion or clarity.

They didn't.

They slipped by quietly, disguised as routine.

There's a particular memory that stays with me.

A child sitting at the kitchen counter, swinging their legs, talking about something that didn't matter.

I don't remember what they were saying.

I remember that they were there.

I remember thinking I should hurry. I had things to do.

I don't remember the task.

I remember the legs swinging.

That's how memory works.

It doesn't keep what we thought was important.

It keeps what felt safe.

We don't think to save ordinary moments because no one tells us they're temporary.

No one warns us that the way a child waits for us now won't always be the way they wait later.

That the unfiltered thoughts won't always be spoken out loud.

That the desire to be near us without a reason will eventually fade.

Not disappear.

Just... move.

Ordinary moments are where children practice being themselves.

Before they edit.

Before they protect.

Before they learn which thoughts to keep quiet.

Those moments are fragile.

Not because they're weak.

Because they're honest.

I remember evenings when nothing happened.

No conflict.

No bonding activity.

Just everyone existing in the same space.

At the time, I thought those evenings were forgettable.

They weren't.

They were the foundation.

We tend to think connection requires intention.

Planning. Focus. Effort.

Sometimes it does.

But often, connection happens in moments we don't recognize as connection.

When we're tired.

When we're distracted.

When we're just there.

There's a difference between doing family time and living

inside it.

Doing it feels deliberate. Structured. Clear.

Living inside it feels unremarkable.

So we overlook it.

Children don't remember whether we planned the moment.

They remember whether we were available inside it.

Whether their voice landed somewhere safe.

Whether their presence felt welcome—or inconvenient.

I think about how often I almost missed these moments.

How easily they could have slipped by without me noticing them at all.

Not because I didn't care.

Because I didn't understand what they were.

There's a quiet sadness in realizing how many meaningful moments feel meaningless while they're happening.

But there's also relief.

Because if you can see that now, it means those moments are still here.

Somewhere in your day.

Waiting quietly.

You might think this chapter is about slowing down.

It's not.

It's about seeing differently.

You don't need more time.

You need a different kind of attention.

The ordinary moments don't need to be protected.

They need to be recognized.

When you see them, they change.

They deepen.

They linger.

There will come a time when you try to remember how it felt

when your child talked without hesitation.

When conversation filled space instead of avoiding it.

When closeness didn't need a reason.

And you'll realize those moments were happening all the time.

You just didn't think to save them.

That realization doesn't have to come later.

It can come now.

Quietly.

Without pressure.

The ordinary moments are already shaping your child's sense of connection.

They're already teaching them whether home is a place where their voice belongs.

Whether presence is easy.

Whether closeness is allowed.

We don't need to turn every moment into something meaningful.

We just need to stop dismissing the ones that already are.

As this chapter ends, notice what feels ordinary today.

The conversation that almost doesn't register.

The presence that feels casual.

The moment that doesn't feel like anything special.

That's where this book begins.

And in the next chapter, we'll talk about the belief that quietly steals those moments away—the idea that we always have more time.

2

I Thought We Had More Time

I thought time was generous.

That's the best way to put it.

Not endless. Just flexible. Forgiving. Something that would stretch when it needed to. Something I could borrow from later if today felt too full.

I didn't think I was wasting time.

I thought I was managing it.

There's a quiet belief many parents carry without ever saying it out loud.

This isn't the season for slowing down.

We tell ourselves that once things settle—once routines stabilize, once work eases, once schedules clear—we'll be more present. More patient. More available.

Later becomes a promise we don't realize we're making.

I remember thinking, *this is just a busy phase.*

School schedules were packed. Days felt short. Evenings blurred. It made sense to postpone certain things—long conversations, unhurried moments, sitting without an agenda.

Not forever.

Just for now.

Now felt temporary.

Time has a way of agreeing with you in the moment.

It lets you believe there will be space later. That the moments you pass over today will return when life is quieter.

And for a while, it seems true.

Tomorrow does look a lot like today.

Until it doesn't.

I used to tell myself I was present enough.

I was there. Physically. Logistically. Responsibly.

I showed up where I needed to. I handled what needed handling.

I thought presence was a box you checked.

I didn't understand that presence has depth.

There were moments I postponed without thinking.

A conversation that started at the wrong time.

A question that came when I was distracted.

A child who wanted attention when I wanted quiet.

I didn't say no outright.

I said *later*.

Later sounded kind. Reasonable. Temporary.

Later is a strange word.

It feels harmless.

It doesn't sound like absence.

It sounds like intention.

I didn't notice how often later appeared in our days.

Later tonight.

Later this weekend.

Later when things slow down.

I thought later meant soon enough.

What I didn't realize was that later was slowly teaching something.

Children learn timing before they learn explanation.

They learn when it's okay to speak.

When to wait.

When to hold a thought back.

Not from rules.

From repetition.

At the time, I thought I was teaching patience.

I didn't realize I was teaching hesitation.

There's a memory that comes back to me sometimes.

A child standing near me, clearly wanting to say something. I noticed it. I really did. I just didn't stop what I was doing.

I remember saying, "Give me a minute."

They nodded.

They waited.

And then... they didn't come back.

Not because they were upset.

Because the moment passed.

That's the part we don't talk about much.

Children don't always circle back.

They don't always hold onto thoughts the way adults do.

Some thoughts exist only in the moment they arrive.

If that moment passes, the thought goes with it.

I didn't realize how many moments were one-time only.

Not big ones.

Small ones.

A reaction.

An idea.

A feeling still forming.

Those don't wait.

I thought we had more time because the days kept repeating.

Breakfast still happened.

School still happened.

Dinner still happened.

On the surface, nothing changed.

Underneath, everything was moving.

Time doesn't announce transitions.

It doesn't warn you when a phase is closing.

One day, a child talks freely.

Another day, they don't.

There's no signpost between those days.

I remember noticing the change without understanding it.

Conversations felt shorter.

Answers more careful.

Questions more selective.

At first, I told myself it was a good thing.

Maturity.

Independence.

And it was.

But it was also something else.

What we call independence often starts as quiet withdrawal.

Not because children don't want us anymore.

Because they're learning what happens when they speak—and when they don't.

I used to think confidence grew from encouragement alone.

Say the right things. Praise effort. Support choices.

Those things matter.

But confidence also grows from timing.

From whether a child feels their thoughts are welcome *right now*—not eventually.

Time, it turns out, isn't generous.

It's precise.

It gives you exactly what it gives you.

And then it moves on.

I don't look back and wish I had done more.

I wish I had delayed less.

Less postponing.

Less assuming.

Less believing there would always be another chance to listen.

The hardest part isn't realizing that time passed.

It's realizing how reasonable it felt to let it pass.

Nothing felt wrong.

Nothing felt urgent.

That's what makes it easy to miss.

I'm not saying we should drop everything every time a child speaks.

That's not real life.

But I am saying this:

The moments we postpone most easily are often the ones that don't come back in the same form.

I thought we had more time because no one tells you when you're running out of a particular kind of closeness.

They don't tell you when the window narrows.

They don't tell you when the door starts closing quietly.

Time doesn't take things away loudly.

It just rearranges what's available.

Looking back, I can see how often I confused *later* with *always*.

I assumed that because something had always been there, it would continue to be.

I didn't realize always has conditions.

If there's anything I want to say clearly here, it's this:

Time doesn't need to be seized.

It needs to be noticed.

You don't have to panic.

You don't have to rush.

You just have to recognize that some moments are asking for you now—not because they're dramatic, but because they're fleeting.

If you're reading this and thinking, *I do this too*, that's not failure.

It's awareness.

And awareness, when it arrives in time, changes what comes next.

In the next chapter, we'll talk about one of the earliest signs that time is shifting—the moment when questions start to slow down, and what that silence is really telling us.

3

When the Questions Slow Down

There was a time when questions filled the space.

N ot politely. Not in order. Just constantly.
Why is that like that?
What happens if...
Can I tell you something?
Do you know why...

They came while I was busy. While I was tired. While my mind was already somewhere else. They arrived without warning and without structure, tumbling out half-formed and urgent, as if they might disappear if they weren't spoken right away.

At the time, it felt overwhelming.

I didn't realize it was closeness.

Questions aren't really about answers.

Not at first.

They're about connection. About testing whether a thought is welcome. About finding out if someone is safe enough to hold an unfinished idea.

Children ask questions when they feel free to think out loud. When they don't yet worry about how something will sound. I remember wishing, more than once, for fewer questions. For quiet.

For space to finish a thought without interruption.

I thought the questions were endless.

They weren't.

The slowing happens quietly.

So quietly that you don't notice it at first.

One day there are fewer *why* questions. Another day, answers come quicker than explanations. Stories get shorter. Thoughts arrive already edited.

It doesn't feel like something is missing.

It feels like growth.

At first, I told myself this was a good thing.

Maturity.

Independence.

Confidence.

And it was.

But it was also a shift.

A turning inward.

Questions are risky.

They expose uncertainty. Curiosity. Confusion.

When children ask questions, they're offering a piece of themselves that isn't finished yet.

That takes trust.

I didn't understand at the time that when questions slowed down, something else was happening too.

Children were learning which questions were worth asking.

And when.

And with whom.

23

There's a difference between a child who has no questions and a child who has learned to keep them to themselves.

That difference isn't obvious.

It shows up slowly.

I think about the questions that used to come out unfiltered.

Questions that wandered. That circled. That didn't quite land anywhere.

Questions that didn't need answers—just space.

Those questions don't disappear.

They just go somewhere else.

Sometimes they go inward.

Sometimes they go to friends.

Sometimes they go unanswered.

There was a moment—I can't remember exactly when—when I realized I hadn't been asked a real question in a while.

Not a logistical one.

Not *Can I go?* or *What time?*

But a question that started in curiosity and ended in vulnerability.

It took me longer than I care to admit to notice.

Silence can look like calm.

It can also look like caution.

I used to think that if a child had a question, they would ask it.

Now I know that isn't always true.

They ask when it feels easy.

When it feels safe.

When it feels like there's room.

Sometimes the room closes without us realizing it.

Not because we intend it to.

Because we're busy. Distracted. Focused on the next thing.

Because we answer quickly instead of listening fully.

Because we postpone without noticing how often.

I remember a question that came late one night.

It started with, "This might be a weird question..."

Those words mattered.

They were a test.

I almost brushed it aside. I was tired. The timing wasn't great.

But something in the hesitation stopped me.

I listened.

I don't remember my answer.

I remember that the question came at all.

There are questions that only arrive once.

Not because the answer is found.

But because the moment to ask passes.

When questions slow down, it doesn't mean children have figured everything out.

It often means they're figuring out where their thoughts belong.

I wish I had understood earlier that questions are a form of trust.

They're an invitation.

Not to respond perfectly.

But to receive.

This chapter isn't about keeping questions coming.

You can't force that.

It's about noticing when they arrive.

About recognizing how much courage lives inside a half-formed thought.

When a child asks a question, they're not just asking for information.

They're asking, *Is this a place I can think out loud?*

If the questions are still coming in your home—even if they

feel constant or inconvenient—that's not something to rush past.

It's something to notice.

Because one day, they slow down.

And you won't hear the last one when it happens.

In the next chapter, we'll talk about what often replaces questions as children grow—and how our instinct to fix things can quietly change the way they share.

4

Listening Without Fixing

Fixing feels helpful.

That's why we do it so quickly. A problem shows up, and our mind starts moving. Solutions line up. Words form before the other person has finished speaking. We interrupt without meaning to. We reassure too soon. We smooth things over before the moment has had time to exist.

It comes from care. From love. From wanting things to be okay.

But listening is slower than fixing.

And slower feels uncomfortable.

When children talk about something hard, our instinct is to make it better.

To explain.

To correct.

To reframe.

We want to lift the weight they're carrying. Sometimes we do it so fast that they never get the chance to set it down themselves.

I didn't notice how often I was fixing until I realized how little silence I allowed.

A child would start talking, and I'd jump in halfway through. Not to shut them down. To help. To guide. To make sense of it for them.

I thought I was being supportive.

I didn't realize I was shortening the moment.

There's a difference between being heard and being handled.

Being heard feels steady.

Being handled feels rushed.

Children know the difference.

I remember a conversation that still lingers with me.

A child was upset about something small. A comment at school. A misunderstanding. Nothing life-altering.

I responded immediately. Explained why it didn't matter. Why it would pass. Why they shouldn't worry.

I thought I was calming them.

What I saw instead was something close.

Not anger.

Not relief.

Withdrawal.

Fixing can quietly signal something we don't intend to say.

It can say, *This is too much.*

Or, *I know better than you.*

Or even, *Let's move past this quickly.*

None of those are what we mean.

But meaning doesn't always land the way we hope.

Listening without fixing feels passive at first.

It feels like doing nothing.

Which is why it's hard.

We're used to measuring care by action.

Silence makes us uneasy.

We worry we're not being helpful. That we're missing an opportunity. That we should say something.

So we fill the space.

But children don't need us to organize their thoughts for them.

They need space to finish them.

I noticed something over time.

When I resisted the urge to fix, conversations lasted longer.

Not because the problem was bigger.

Because the trust was.

There's a moment in every conversation when a child pauses.

That pause matters.

It's where they decide whether to keep going.

If we rush in there—if we solve or soften or redirect—we take that decision away from them.

Listening without fixing doesn't mean staying silent forever.

It means waiting long enough to understand what the moment actually needs.

Sometimes it needs words.

Sometimes it just needs room.

I used to think good parenting meant having good answers.

I'm learning it often means having good patience.

There were times I felt proud of how quickly I could help.

How efficiently I could turn a hard moment into a manageable one.

Now I wonder how many conversations ended early because I did that.

Not ended badly.

Just ended sooner than they needed to.

Children don't always want solutions.

They want confirmation that their feelings make sense.

That their experience is real.

That they don't have to rush past it.

Fixing can close a door gently.

Listening keeps it open.

I think about the difference between saying, "You'll be fine," and saying nothing at all.

Silence, when it's attentive, can feel like permission.

Permission to keep talking.

Permission to stay with a feeling.

Permission to exist as they are in that moment.

There's a kind of listening that says, *I'm here, and I'm not going anywhere.*

It doesn't rush the ending.

It doesn't tidy the story.

It lets the moment breathe.

This chapter isn't about never helping.

It's about noticing how quickly we reach for solutions when what's being asked for is presence.

Listening without fixing takes restraint.

It asks us to sit with discomfort.

To trust that not every moment needs to be smoothed out.

To believe that children can carry their own thoughts when given space.

I don't think I learned this all at once.

I think I learned it by watching what happened when I said less.

When I waited.

When I let silence do some of the work.

The conversations didn't become heavier.

They became deeper.

In the next chapter, we'll talk about what happens when moments end without warning—and how some of the most meaningful ones slip away before we realize they're gone.

5

The Last Time You Didn't Know Was the Last Time

The last time rarely announces itself.

I t doesn't pause.
   It doesn't warn you.
   It doesn't ask you to pay attention.
It looks exactly like all the other times.

That's what makes it hard.

If the last time felt different—heavier, clearer, marked with emotion—we would catch it. We would slow down. We would stay a little longer.

But the last time feels ordinary.

That's why it gets missed.

I don't remember the last bedtime story I read out loud.

I remember reading stories. Hundreds of them. Sitting on the edge of the bed. Turning pages. Skipping parts. Rushing some nights. Lingering on others.

But the last one?

I didn't know it was happening.

I thought there would be another night. Another request. Another *just one more*.

There wasn't.

That's how endings arrive in families.

Quietly.

Without ceremony.

Disguised as routine.

There was a time when my children reached for my hand without thinking.

Crossing the street. Walking through a parking lot. Sitting next to me just because.

I noticed when it happened.

I didn't notice when it stopped.

Endings don't arrive as moments.

They arrive as absences.

You notice them later—when you reach for something that isn't there anymore.

There's a particular kind of grief that comes from realizing you were present for the last time, but unaware of its meaning.

It isn't dramatic.

It's soft.

It feels like delayed understanding.

I think about how many *lasts* pass through a home unnoticed.

The last time a child climbs into your lap without hesitation.

The last time they narrate their entire day.

The last time they ask you to sit with them just because.

None of those moments ask to be saved.

So we don't save them.

It isn't that we take them for granted.

It's that we assume continuity.

We assume repetition.

We assume tomorrow will look close enough to today.

There's comfort in that assumption.

It lets us move through life without constant awareness.

But it also blinds us to transition.

I remember a morning routine that repeated for years.

Same time. Same rhythm. Same small interactions.

Then one morning, it didn't happen.

Not because of a decision.

Because of growth.

Schedules shifted. Independence arrived. The routine dissolved without discussion.

I didn't mourn it then.

I noticed it later.

That's when the weight landed.

Not when it ended.

When I realized it had ended.

We don't notice endings because we aren't meant to live in constant anticipation of loss.

That would be exhausting.

But there's something about family life that deserves a different kind of attention.

Not vigilance.

Presence.

The hardest part about the last time is that it doesn't feel important until it's gone.

And by then, you can't go back.

I used to think memory worked like a camera.

That it captured what stood out.

I've learned it works more like a feeling.

It keeps what mattered emotionally, not what looked significant.

The memories that stay aren't always the big ones.

They're the ones that felt safe. Repetitive. Ordinary.

The ones you didn't know you were collecting.

I think about how often we say *later* without realizing we're saying *maybe never*.

Not intentionally.

Just casually.

There was a night when a child hovered near me, clearly wanting something.

I noticed. I really did.

I said, "In a minute."

That minute turned into something else.

That something else turned into bedtime.

That moment never came back in the same way.

Nothing went wrong.

That's what makes it easy to overlook.

When people talk about missing childhood, they often mean the big things.

I think what they miss most are the small, repetitive moments that quietly shaped their days.

The predictability.

The closeness without effort.

The way connection didn't have to be planned.

Children grow out of certain forms of closeness not because they stop loving us.

Because they're supposed to.

And when that happens, the old versions don't come back.

They're replaced.

But replacement isn't the same as return.

There's a tenderness in realizing how many endings pass

through a family unnoticed.

It doesn't mean we failed.

It means we were living.

I don't write this to create sadness.

I write it to create awareness.

Because awareness—when it arrives in time—changes what we notice.

You don't need to catch every last time.

That isn't possible.

But you can begin seeing moments more clearly while they're still happening.

The goal isn't to freeze time.

It's to feel it.

If you're reading this and thinking about something that used to happen in your home that doesn't anymore, you're not alone.

That recognition connects parents more than anything else.

The last time doesn't ask to be honored.

But we can honor the moments that are still repeating.

By staying present.

By lingering when we can.

By not rushing past what feels ordinary.

Because one day, those ordinary moments will stop repeating.

And you won't know it when they do.

What you *can* know is this:

Right now, there are moments in your life that feel routine, predictable, almost forgettable.

Those are the ones shaping everything.

In the next chapter, we'll talk about how family time often looks different from what we imagined—and why letting go of expectations can help us see what's actually there.

6

Family Time Doesn't Look Like We Imagined

When I pictured family time, I imagined something clear.

Everyone together.
Everyone engaged.
Everyone enjoying the same thing at the same time.

I thought it would be obvious when it was happening.

It turns out that picture made it harder to see what was actually there.

Family time, as it exists in real life, is rarely neat.

It's uneven. Distracted. Sometimes quiet in ways that feel uncomfortable. Sometimes loud in ways that feel chaotic.

It doesn't pause so you can label it.

I used to wait for the *right* version of family time.

A free evening.

A shared activity.

A moment when everyone seemed willing and present.

If the moment didn't look like that, I told myself it didn't count.

There were nights when everyone was in the same room, doing different things.

Someone reading.

Someone scrolling.

Someone pacing.

I thought those moments were missed opportunities.

I didn't realize they were already moments.

Family time doesn't always announce itself with laughter or conversation.

Sometimes it looks like coexistence.

Like choosing the same space without needing the same focus.

I think a lot of parents carry quiet disappointment about family time.

They imagine something warmer. More connected. More meaningful.

And when reality doesn't match that image, they assume they're doing something wrong.

I've learned that expectations can quietly blind us.

They make us look for a specific shape.

And when connection doesn't take that shape, we miss it.

There were afternoons when my children sat near me, not talking.

Just there.

At the time, I wondered if I should initiate something. Ask questions. Create interaction.

Now I understand that presence without performance is its own form of closeness.

Children don't always want to engage.

Sometimes they want to be near.

That's a different request.

I used to think family time required intention.

Planning. Energy. Structure.

Sometimes it does.

But some of the most meaningful moments happen when no one is trying.

There's a difference between shared activity and shared space.

Both matter.

But shared space is easier to overlook.

Because it feels passive.

I remember thinking that if we weren't talking, we weren't connecting.

Silence felt like a failure.

Now I see silence differently.

Silence, when it's comfortable, means something is settled.

It means no one needs to perform.

It means being together doesn't require effort.

Family time often happens sideways.

In glances.

In small comments.

In the way a child chooses to stay nearby instead of going somewhere else.

Those moments don't look impressive.

They don't feel productive.

But they build something steady underneath.

I've noticed that the moments children remember later aren't always the ones we planned.

They remember the feeling of being allowed to exist without explanation.

The evenings that felt unremarkable.

The presence that wasn't rushed.

We sometimes chase connection so hard that we overlook the

version already happening.

We try to create moments instead of noticing them.

I think it's easy to confuse effort with value.

If it takes planning, we assume it matters more.

If it happens naturally, we assume it matters less.

Family time works the opposite way.

Some of the strongest moments happen when nothing is happening.

No agenda.

No expectation.

No outcome.

Just time passing gently.

There were times I thought I needed to do more.

More activities. More conversations. More structure.

What I needed was to interrupt less.

Family time doesn't need to be curated.

It needs to be allowed.

When we release the picture of what family time *should* look like, something softens.

We stop evaluating moments as successes or failures.

We start noticing what's actually there.

Not every evening will feel connected.

Not every moment will feel meaningful.

That's not the point.

The point is recognizing that connection doesn't require perfection.

I wish I had understood earlier that family time is less about alignment and more about availability.

About being someone a child can sit near without pressure.

Someone who doesn't require the moment to look a certain way.

Family time doesn't need to match the image in our heads.

It needs to match the reality of our lives.

Messy.

Full.

Uneven.

Real.

When we stop chasing an ideal version, we make room for the one that's already happening.

And that version counts more than we think.

In the next chapter, we'll talk about busyness—the kind that comes from love and responsibility—and why being busy doesn't mean being disconnected.

7

Busy Doesn't Mean You Don't Care

Busy has a bad reputation.

I t gets blamed for everything—distance, disconnection, missed moments, the feeling that time keeps slipping through our hands.

But most parents I know aren't busy because they're avoiding their families.

They're busy because they're trying to take care of them.

Busy often comes from love.

From responsibility.

From wanting to provide.

From wanting to get things right.

It doesn't come from indifference.

I remember days when everything felt full.

Calendars packed. Tasks overlapping. One thing bleeding into the next without pause.

I didn't feel careless during those days.

I felt stretched.

There's a difference between being busy and being unavailable.

They can look similar on the surface.

They aren't the same.

I used to worry that busyness automatically meant I was missing something important.

That if I wasn't fully present all the time, I was failing.

That belief carried more guilt than clarity.

Busyness doesn't cancel care.

But it can crowd it.

There were evenings when I was physically present but mentally elsewhere.

Not because I didn't want to be there.

Because my mind was still trying to finish the day.

That kind of distraction is quiet.

It doesn't look like absence.

But children feel it.

At the same time, there were days I worried too much about balance.

About doing enough. About being enough.

That worry didn't make me more present.

It made me tense.

Children don't need us calm and perfect.

They need us human.

I've learned that busyness becomes a problem when it never loosens its grip.

When there's no room for pause.

No margin for interruption.

No space for something unplanned to matter.

But being busy doesn't mean you don't care.

It means life is asking something of you.

Often for good reasons.

I think parents are harder on themselves than they need to be.

We carry quiet narratives about what we should be doing.

How we should be showing up.

How much time should be enough.

Time isn't always something we can control.

But attention often is.

There were moments when I couldn't slow the pace of the day.

But I could slow my response.

I could look up.

I could stay for one more sentence.

Those moments didn't require less busyness.

They required a small shift inside it.

Busy doesn't have to mean rushed.

I remember a child talking to me while I gathered things to leave.

I didn't stop what I was doing.

But I stayed in the conversation.

I listened fully, even while moving.

That mattered.

Presence doesn't always look still.

Sometimes it looks engaged.

We tend to measure connection by quantity.

How long we sit. How much time we give.

Children often measure it by quality.

By whether they feel received when they speak.

Busy days can still hold connection.

If we let them.

The danger isn't being busy.

It's believing busyness excuses us from noticing.

I used to think I needed large stretches of uninterrupted time to connect.

Now I see how much can happen in fragments.

In short conversations.

In quick check-ins.

In moments we don't label as meaningful.

Busyness doesn't erase those moments.

Inattention does.

I don't believe the answer is doing less.

I believe the answer is seeing more.

Seeing what's already happening.

Seeing how much connection is woven into ordinary days if we allow it to surface.

Parents who care worry about busyness.

Parents who don't care don't notice it at all.

If you're busy, that doesn't disqualify you.

It places you in the reality most families live in.

The goal isn't to eliminate busyness.

It's to soften it.

To let moments breathe inside it.

Busy doesn't mean you don't care.

It means you're carrying a lot.

And carrying a lot deserves compassion.

In the next chapter, we'll talk about the subtle moment when the house starts to feel different—and what that quiet shift often signals.

8

The House Feels Different Now

It's hard to explain the moment you notice it.

Nothing dramatic happens.
Nothing breaks.
Nothing goes wrong.
The house just feels... different.
At first, I thought it was my imagination.
The same rooms.
The same furniture.
The same routines.
But something had shifted underneath it all.
The noise level changed.
Not suddenly. Gradually.
There were fewer voices calling out from room to room. Fewer running footsteps. Fewer interruptions that once felt constant.
The quiet didn't feel empty.
It felt unfamiliar.
I remember standing in the kitchen one afternoon, noticing

how still everything felt.

No one needed anything right then.

No one was asking questions.

No one was hovering nearby.

It should have felt peaceful.

Instead, it felt noticeable.

When children are younger, the house feels alive in a particular way.

Messy. Loud. Demanding.

You don't always enjoy it while it's happening.

But it fills the space.

As children grow, that fullness changes.

They spend more time behind closed doors. Conversations move elsewhere. Energy turns inward.

The house doesn't lose life.

It changes rhythm.

I didn't realize how much I relied on the old rhythm until it softened.

The background noise I once rushed through had been grounding me without my realizing it.

There's a moment many parents experience but don't talk about much.

The moment you realize the house no longer revolves around you in the same way.

Children move through it with more independence. More intention. Less need.

It's healthy.

And still... tender.

I used to think I would notice this transition clearly.

That there would be a specific day when I could say, *This is different now.*

There wasn't.

It crept in quietly.

The signs were small.

A door that stayed closed a little longer.

A meal eaten more quickly.

A conversation that happened later—or not at all.

None of it felt alarming.

It just accumulated.

I noticed that evenings felt longer.

Not because there was more time.

Because there was less interruption.

At first, I welcomed it.

More space. More quiet. More room to think.

But then I realized what had changed.

The house wasn't quieter because there was nothing to say.

It was quieter because more was happening internally.

Children don't stop needing us when the house gets quieter.

They stop needing us loudly.

I think that's what makes this phase confusing.

We associate need with noise.

When the noise fades, we assume the need has faded too.

It hasn't.

It's just taken a different form.

I remember waiting for the sounds I used to find distracting.

The constant narration.

The casual interruptions.

The small requests that pulled me out of my thoughts.

I didn't realize how much they connected me to the rhythm of family life.

When those sounds faded, the house felt less demanding.

But also less anchoring.

49

There's a grief in realizing a phase has ended without saying goodbye.

Not because it was perfect.

But because it was familiar.

I don't think we talk enough about this quiet transition.

About how strange it feels to miss something you once wanted space from.

The house feels different now because the relationship has changed.

Not worse.

Just changed.

Children learn to hold more of themselves privately as they grow.

They test independence. They protect their inner world. They practice being separate.

That isn't distance.

It's development.

But development still leaves an echo.

I noticed I had to listen differently.

I couldn't rely on constant cues anymore.

I had to pay attention to what wasn't being said.

To timing.

To tone.

To presence.

The house teaches you this lesson quietly.

You don't get instructions.

You get atmosphere.

I think back to how much the house once reflected our closeness.

How noise once equaled connection.

Now I see that connection doesn't disappear when the noise

does.

It just asks for a different kind of attention.

When the house feels different, it's easy to assume you've missed your chance.

That something has slipped away for good.

That isn't true.

The shift doesn't mean closeness is gone.

It means closeness needs to be approached differently.

I wish I had known that earlier.

That the quiet wasn't rejection.

It was growth.

The house doesn't stop holding family time when it changes.

It just stops presenting it the same way.

If your house feels different now, you're not alone.

That feeling connects more parents than we admit.

It's a sign of transition.

Not an ending.

In the next chapter, we'll talk about what children actually remember about home—and why it's often different from what we think.

9

What Children Remember About Home

Children don't remember homes the way adults do.

They don't catalogue square footage or furniture or how clean things were on an average Tuesday. They don't measure success by routines followed perfectly or rules enforced consistently.

They remember how it felt to be there.

I used to think children would remember the things I worried about most.

Whether I said the right thing.

Whether I handled moments correctly.

Whether I balanced everything the way I was supposed to.

What I see now is that those details fade.

The feeling stays.

Home, for a child, is less a place and more an atmosphere.

It's the tone of conversations.

The way mistakes are handled.

The feeling in the room when they walk in.

WHAT CHILDREN REMEMBER ABOUT HOME

It's whether their presence feels natural—or disruptive.

Children remember whether they could speak freely.

Not whether every word was met with agreement, but whether it was met with attention.

They remember if they felt rushed.

Or received.

Or quietly tolerated.

I think we overestimate how much children remember what we say.

And underestimate how deeply they remember how we respond.

There are moments I don't remember clearly.

Specific conversations. Exact words.

But I remember how the house felt at certain times of the day.

Calm.

Tense.

Open.

Heavy.

Those feelings lingered longer than any single interaction.

Children build their sense of safety from patterns.

Not from one perfect day.

But from the accumulation of small moments that teach them what to expect.

I used to believe children would remember the effort.

The planning.

The juggling.

The sacrifices.

They don't.

They remember the availability.

Availability isn't about being there all the time.

It's about being accessible when it matters.

When a thought surfaces.

When a feeling needs space.

When something unfinished needs somewhere to land.

I think about the homes people describe fondly later in life.

They don't say, *It was well organized.*

They say things like:

"I always felt welcome."

"It was okay to talk."

"I knew where I stood."

Those are emotional memories.

They don't come from perfection.

They come from consistency.

Children remember whether home felt like a place they could return to emotionally.

Even as they grew older.

Even as they became more independent.

They remember whether the door stayed open—not physically, but relationally.

I've noticed that children often remember the tone of correction more than the correction itself.

Whether mistakes were met with curiosity or impatience.

Whether disappointment felt like distance—or discussion.

Home teaches children what to expect from relationships.

Not through instruction.

Through repetition.

I used to think confidence came from encouragement alone.

From praise. From support. From affirmation.

Those things matter.

But confidence is also built quietly, in the background.

In whether a child feels their voice belongs.

In whether home feels like a place they can think out loud.

Children remember whether silence felt safe.

Whether being quiet meant peace—or tension.

Whether stillness felt like comfort—or avoidance.

I think about the way children retreat when they don't feel emotionally received.

Not dramatically.

Subtly.

They share less.

They explain less.

They protect more.

That retreat doesn't always come from conflict.

It often comes from accumulation.

From moments when a child felt unseen or rushed—not once, but enough times to learn a pattern.

Home doesn't have to be perfect to be remembered in the right way.

It has to be emotionally predictable.

Predictable doesn't mean rigid.

It means consistent.

I've learned that children carry home with them long after they leave it.

Not the layout.

The feeling.

They remember whether home was a place they could exhale.

Whether they could arrive as they were.

Whether their presence felt like a contribution—not a complication.

Those memories don't fade.

They shape how children approach the world.

How they speak up.

How they trust.

How they connect.

I wish I had worried less about getting things right and more about being emotionally steady.

Not perfect.

Steady.

Home is remembered less for what happened there and more for how it held what happened.

If you're wondering what your children will remember, the answer isn't found in your calendar or your accomplishments.

It's found in the atmosphere you create when nothing special is happening.

Children remember the feeling of being welcomed.

Of being heard.

Of being allowed to exist without performance.

That feeling becomes part of them.

It travels with them.

It shows up in how they treat themselves—and others.

Home, in that way, never really leaves.

In the next chapter, we'll talk about the quiet power of simply sitting together—and why presence without conversation often matters more than we expect.

10

The Power of Sitting Together

There's a kind of togetherness we don't talk about much.

It doesn't involve conversation.
It doesn't involve eye contact.
It doesn't even involve doing the same thing.
It's just sitting.
I used to think time together had to be filled.
With words.
With questions.
With activities.
If nothing was happening, I assumed something was missing.
Then I noticed how often my children chose to sit near me without saying anything.
On the couch while I read.
At the table while I worked.
In the same room, doing their own thing.
They weren't asking for attention.
They were asking for proximity.

At first, that kind of closeness felt confusing.

Should I engage?

Start a conversation?

Make it meaningful somehow?

I didn't realize it already was.

Sitting together without talking can feel awkward for adults.

We're used to filling space.

Children aren't.

For them, shared silence can feel safe.

I remember evenings when no one spoke for long stretches.

I thought those evenings were forgettable.

They weren't.

They were calm.

There's something grounding about knowing someone is there, even if you're not interacting.

It creates a sense of steadiness.

Of being anchored.

Children don't always want to explain themselves.

Sometimes they just want to be near someone who feels familiar.

Someone who doesn't need them to perform.

I think about how often adults measure connection by conversation.

How much we talked.

How deep it went.

What was said.

Children often measure it by presence.

By whether someone stayed.

Sitting together sends a quiet message.

You don't have to entertain me.

You don't have to explain yourself.

You don't have to be "on."

Just be here.

I noticed that when I stopped trying to turn every quiet moment into something productive, those moments became more frequent.

Children stayed longer.

They lingered.

There's a comfort in knowing you can exist alongside someone without effort.

That kind of comfort doesn't come from interaction.

It comes from consistency.

I used to underestimate how much children absorb in these moments.

They notice tone.

Energy.

Whether you seem rushed—or settled.

Even when no words are exchanged.

Sitting together creates a background sense of connection.

It doesn't demand anything.

It just holds space.

I think this is why children sometimes leave a room when it feels tense, even if nothing is said.

And why they stay when it feels calm.

They're reading the atmosphere.

There were times I felt guilty for not engaging more.

For not turning those moments into conversations or activities.

Now I see that I was already giving something valuable.

Presence without pressure is rare.

And powerful.

We don't always need to talk to stay connected.

Sometimes talking interrupts something quieter.

Children often return to rooms where they feel allowed to just be.

Not asked questions.

Not corrected.

Not guided.

Just welcomed.

I think about how different this feels from adult relationships.

We're trained to fill silence.

Children haven't learned that yet.

They don't see silence as absence.

They see it as space.

Sitting together teaches children something important.

That closeness doesn't require effort.

That connection doesn't always need words.

That being near someone can be enough.

Those lessons stay.

They show up later in how comfortable someone is with themselves.

With others.

With quiet.

I wish I had trusted these moments sooner.

Instead of wondering if I was doing enough.

The power of sitting together isn't obvious.

It doesn't announce itself.

It doesn't look meaningful.

But it builds something steady underneath.

If your child sits near you without saying anything, resist the urge to fill the space.

Let it be.

That moment is already doing its work.

In the next chapter, we'll talk about what happens when children start turning away—not in rejection, but in growth—and how that shift can feel more complicated than we expect.

11

When Children Start Turning Away

It doesn't happen all at once.

There's no announcement.
No conversation where someone explains what's changing.
Children just start turning away a little more often.
At first, it's subtle.
They stay in their room longer.
They answer questions more briefly.
They seem content not being nearby.
You notice it, but you don't know what to do with the feeling.
So you tell yourself it's normal.
Because it is.
Turning away is part of growing.
Children are meant to separate. To experiment with independence. To build an inner world that belongs to them.
That doesn't make it easy to witness.
I remember the first time I felt it clearly.

The moment I realized I wasn't the default anymore.

Not the first person they turned to.

Not the automatic place for every thought.

It didn't feel like rejection.

It felt like displacement.

I remember standing in the hallway one evening, hearing a door close softly instead of a voice calling my name.

Not slammed. Not angry. Just closed.

Nothing was wrong.

But something had shifted, and I felt it before I understood it.

Parents don't talk much about this part.

About how confusing it feels to be needed differently.

Not less.

Just differently.

When children are small, their closeness is constant.

They orbit you.

As they grow, that orbit widens.

They move farther out.

They come back—but not as often, and not without intention.

I used to mistake turning away for distance.

Now I understand it as development.

Still, understanding doesn't erase the feeling.

There's a quiet fear that creeps in during this phase.

Did I miss something?

Did I do something wrong?

Is this permanent?

Those questions don't always get answers.

Children don't turn away because we failed them.

They turn away because they're learning how to stand on their own.

That process requires space.

What makes this phase hard is that it asks parents to do something counterintuitive.

To stay open without chasing.

To be available without insisting.

To remain steady without pulling them back in.

I noticed that when I tried to close the distance, it widened.

When I asked too many questions, answers shortened.

When I hovered, space increased.

Turning away isn't an invitation to withdraw.

It's an invitation to adjust.

Children at this stage are testing something important.

Whether closeness can exist without pressure.

Whether they can come and go without consequence.

Whether home remains safe even when they're not constantly present.

I learned that the most helpful response wasn't to pull them closer.

It was to stay where I was.

Emotionally available.

Unchanged.

Open.

There's something powerful about being someone a child can return to without explanation.

No interrogation.

No disappointment.

No guilt.

Just familiarity.

When children start turning away, parents often feel the urge to hold tighter.

To reassert connection.

To make sure nothing is slipping.

That instinct comes from love.

But it can send the wrong signal.

Closeness that's demanded feels different from closeness that's chosen.

Children know that.

I remember moments when my instinct was to comment.

To point out the distance.

To name the change.

To say, "You don't talk to me like you used to."

I'm glad I didn't.

Those words can turn growth into pressure.

Turning away doesn't mean children don't care.

It means they're expanding.

What they need most during this time isn't more closeness.

It's reassurance that closeness is still there.

Unconditional.

Untouched.

Waiting.

The house might feel quieter during this phase.

The space might feel larger.

That doesn't mean something is missing.

It means something is shifting.

Parents who stay steady through this shift become anchors.

Not by pulling children back.

But by remaining consistent enough for children to return when they're ready.

I think this is one of the hardest parts of parenting.

Learning when to step back without stepping away.

If your child is turning away right now, try not to see it as an ending.

See it as movement.

Movement doesn't erase connection.

It changes its shape.

In the next chapter, we'll talk about how family time evolves as children grow—and how letting go of old expectations can make room for new forms of closeness.

12

Family Time Changes, Not Disappears

For a long time, I thought family time had a single shape.

Everyone together.

Everyone talking.

Everyone present in the same way.

When that shape started to fade, I worried we were losing something.

What I see now is that we weren't losing it.

It was changing.

Family time doesn't end when children grow.

It transforms.

And transformation can feel like loss when you're still looking for the old version.

There was a period when I kept waiting for things to return to how they were.

Longer conversations.

Spontaneous closeness.

The kind of togetherness that didn't require planning.

I didn't realize I was waiting for a phase that had already done its work.

Children don't carry family time forward unchanged.

They carry it differently.

What once looked like constant interaction becomes something quieter.

More selective.

More intentional.

I began to notice that connection started happening in shorter windows.

A comment in passing.

A shared glance.

A brief exchange that meant more than it looked like.

Those moments didn't linger.

They landed.

Family time, as children grow, often shows up when you're not looking for it.

Late at night.

In the car.

In between activities.

It doesn't announce itself.

It slips in.

One night, I was driving, thinking about something else entirely, when a quiet comment came from the passenger seat.

It wasn't a question. It wasn't even clearly directed at me.

I answered it anyway, gently, without turning it into a conversation.

The car went quiet again—but something settled in that space.

I used to think family time needed to be protected from change.

Now I see it needs to be flexible enough to survive it.

There's a temptation to hold on tightly to old rituals.

To insist they remain unchanged.

But closeness that's forced loses its ease.

It becomes effort instead of comfort.

Letting go of old expectations made room for something new.

Something more age-appropriate.

Something that respected who my children were becoming.

Family time in later years doesn't look like constant togetherness.

It looks like trust.

Like knowing when to show up—and when to step back.

Like understanding that closeness doesn't need to be visible to be real.

I noticed that when I stopped trying to recreate the past, I became more present in the present.

I stopped comparing.

I started noticing.

There's a quiet confidence that develops when children know connection hasn't disappeared—only shifted.

That they're allowed to grow without losing access to home.

Family time becomes less about shared activities and more about shared understanding.

About knowing you're welcome.

About knowing you can return.

I think that's one of the greatest gifts parents give without realizing it.

A sense of continuity.

That even as everything changes, some things remain steady.

The earlier versions of family time don't vanish.

They become part of the foundation.

They support what comes next.

I used to think change meant loss.

Now I see it as evolution.

And evolution doesn't erase what came before.

It builds on it.

If you're in a stage where family time looks unfamiliar, resist the urge to label it as less.

Different doesn't mean diminished.

Connection matures.

It becomes quieter.

It asks for trust instead of proximity.

Family time changes because families change.

That's not something to fear.

It's something to understand.

When you allow family time to evolve, you make it sustainable.

You make room for growth without rupture.

You keep the door open.

And that door matters more than any single moment ever did.

In the next chapter, we'll talk about something parents rarely hear enough of—the truth that you're likely doing better than you think.

13

You're Doing Better Than You Think

Most parents don't give themselves much credit.

We notice what we missed.
What we rushed.
What we wish we had done differently.

We rarely notice what held.

I've spent a lot of time thinking about the quiet weight parents carry.

The invisible tally.

The constant self-checking.

The unspoken question of whether we're doing enough.

It's exhausting.

I used to replay moments in my head.

Things I could have said better.

Times I could have stayed longer.

Conversations I could have handled differently.

I told myself this reflection made me more careful.

What it really made me was heavier.

Parents often assume that if something feels hard, they must be doing it wrong.

That ease would mean success.

That struggle means failure.

Neither of those things is true.

Caring deeply makes everything feel harder.

Not easier.

I didn't realize how much effort went unseen.

The consistency.

The showing up.

The emotional steadiness required day after day.

Children don't announce when these things matter.

They absorb them quietly.

There were days I felt scattered.

Pulled in different directions.

Unsure if I was meeting anyone's needs well.

I thought children noticed my uncertainty.

What they noticed was my presence.

I remember a morning when everything felt rushed, nothing done particularly well.

Later that day, a child sat nearby without asking for anything, just close enough to be felt.

No reassurance was requested. No review of the morning was needed.

That quiet return told me more than any perfect response ever could.

We underestimate how forgiving children can be when they feel loved.

They don't expect perfection.

They expect reliability.

I've learned that children don't need flawless parents.

They need predictable ones.

Parents who respond in familiar ways.

Parents whose tone feels safe.

Parents who repair when things go wrong.

Repair matters more than precision.

I think about how often parents apologize for being busy.

For being tired.

For not having endless patience.

Children don't measure love that way.

They measure it by whether they feel secure.

I remember standing in a doorway once, about to explain myself.

To justify the short answer. To soften the tone after the fact.

I didn't. And nothing broke.

Security doesn't come from getting everything right.

It comes from knowing the relationship holds even when things aren't smooth.

There's a misconception that good parenting feels confident.

In reality, it often feels uncertain.

Because caring makes you question yourself.

If you're worried about whether you're doing enough, that worry itself is a sign of investment.

Parents who don't care don't ask these questions.

I wish someone had told me sooner that self-criticism doesn't improve connection.

It tightens it.

Children don't need us to be harder on ourselves.

They need us to be present with them.

I've noticed that when parents soften toward themselves, something changes in the home.

The atmosphere relaxes.

The pressure lifts.

Conversations feel less guarded.

Children sense when we're constantly judging ourselves.

They learn that tone.

They absorb that standard.

Offering yourself compassion isn't indulgent.

It's protective.

You don't have to erase mistakes to be doing well.

You have to show up again.

I think about the moments I once dismissed as insignificant.

The quick check-ins.

The shared glances.

The calm responses when things could have escalated.

Those moments mattered more than I knew.

Parents tend to focus on what they didn't give.

Children often remember what they did receive.

There's a quiet steadiness that forms when children grow up feeling emotionally received.

It doesn't come from dramatic gestures.

It comes from accumulation.

You may not feel like you're doing enough.

That doesn't mean you aren't.

Parenting isn't judged in real time.

Its effects show up later.

In how children trust.

In how they speak up.

In how they return.

If your child still feels comfortable being near you—even occasionally—that's not accidental.

It's built.

If they still come to you with parts of themselves, even small ones, that's not luck.

It's earned.

I wish more parents understood this:

Doing better doesn't always feel like success.

Sometimes it feels like doubt.

Sometimes it feels like fatigue.

Sometimes it feels like caring more than you can comfortably hold.

Those feelings don't disqualify you.

They confirm your investment.

You don't need to become a better parent.

You need to recognize the parent you already are.

When you stop measuring yourself against an imagined ideal, you can see what's actually happening.

Connection.

Trust.

Continuity.

Those things don't show up on checklists.

They show up in relationships.

If you're reading this and feeling unsure, that doesn't mean you're behind.

It means you're engaged.

You're doing better than you think.

And that realization changes how you move forward.

In the next chapter, we'll talk about the moments that still count—especially the small ones that are easy to overlook even now.

14

The Moments That Still Count

It's easy to believe that the most important moments are behind you.

Than the best chances for closeness have already passed. That what remains is smaller. Thinner. Less meaningful.

That belief isn't true.

There are moments that still count.

They just don't look the way they used to.

I used to think meaningful moments arrived loudly.

With emotion.

With conversation.

With some clear signal that said, *pay attention.*

Now I know many of them arrive quietly.

Almost unnoticed.

A brief check-in.

A shared glance.

A comment made in passing that lands deeper than expected.

Those moments don't linger.

But they stay.

As children grow, moments of connection become more selective.

Less frequent.

But often more precise.

I remember realizing that conversations had shifted.

They weren't constant anymore.

They arrived unexpectedly.

Late at night.

In the car.

In between activities.

I had to learn to be ready when they showed up.

The moments that still count don't wait for ideal timing.

They appear when there's room.

Room we either notice—or don't.

I think we underestimate how much impact small moments still have.

A calm response instead of a quick correction.

A pause before reacting.

A willingness to listen even when the timing isn't perfect.

Those moments still shape trust.

There's a temptation to believe that if we missed earlier chances, it's too late now.

That belief creates distance where none needs to exist.

Connection doesn't have an expiration date.

It changes form.

I've noticed that children often test connection quietly as they grow.

They offer small openings.

A comment.

A question that doesn't sound like a question.

A presence that lingers briefly.

Those openings are easy to miss because they're subtle.

I remember reading a message that appeared on my phone late in the evening—nothing urgent, nothing dramatic.

Just a few words, sent without explanation.

I responded simply, resisting the urge to ask for more.

The exchange ended there, but the connection stayed.

The moments that still count require attentiveness, not effort.

They ask for availability, not performance.

I used to think I needed to create moments.

Now I see how often they arrive on their own.

They just need space.

A child sitting nearby longer than necessary.

A conversation that begins with humor and ends somewhere serious.

A shared silence that feels settled instead of awkward.

Those moments still build something important.

They tell children that connection is still possible.

That closeness hasn't disappeared.

That home is still a place they can return to emotionally.

I think about how powerful it is for a child to feel they can approach without pressure.

Without expectation.

Without needing to explain why.

The moments that still count aren't dramatic.

They're dependable.

They show children that connection doesn't require intensity.

It requires consistency.

Even now, there are moments unfolding that you might not recognize as meaningful.

Because they feel ordinary.

Because they don't last long.

Because they don't announce themselves.

Those moments count.

They count because they reinforce something steady.

They say, *I'm here.*

They say, *You matter.*

They say, *This relationship still holds.*

I've learned that it's never too late to notice.

Notice tone.

Notice timing.

Notice the small openings that appear without warning.

You don't need to recreate the past.

You need to respond to the present.

The moments that still count often arrive when you're not expecting them.

When you're tired.

When you're distracted.

When you're almost finished with something else.

If you can stay just a little longer in those moments, they deepen.

They don't need to be extended.

They just need to be acknowledged.

I think that's one of the quiet truths of family life.

Connection doesn't disappear.

It waits.

The moments that still count are happening now.

They're happening in between everything else.

They're small enough to overlook—and strong enough to shape what comes next.

In the next chapter, we'll talk about what stays after childhood moves on—and how the meaning of family time carries forward in ways we don't always see.

15

What Stays After Childhood Moves On

Childhood doesn't leave all at once.

I t fades in layers.
One habit at a time.
One routine at a time.
One version of closeness quietly replaced by another.
What remains isn't always visible.
But it's there.
When children grow, it can feel like so much is moving forward that nothing is staying behind.
Schedules change.
Conversations shift.
Independence expands.
It's easy to focus on what's gone.
Harder to notice what's stayed.
I used to think family time mattered only while childhood was actively unfolding.
That once children grew past a certain stage, those moments

stopped doing their work.

I see now how wrong that was.

Family time doesn't end when childhood moves on.

It settles.

It becomes part of how children understand themselves and the world.

What stays isn't the specific moments.

It's the emotional imprint they left.

The sense of being welcome.

The expectation of being heard.

The confidence that connection is available, even when it's not constant.

I think about how people describe their families years later.

They don't recount every interaction.

They talk about how it felt to be there.

Whether they felt understood.

Whether they felt safe.

Whether they felt supported without being controlled.

Those feelings don't fade with age.

They become reference points.

Children carry family time with them in subtle ways.

In how they approach conversations.

In how comfortable they are with silence.

In how easily they trust that relationships can hold complexity.

I've noticed that children who grow up feeling emotionally received don't need constant reassurance later.

They move through the world with a quieter confidence.

Not loud.

Steady.

What stays is the tone we set over years.

The emotional climate we maintained without always realizing it.

The sense that home was a place where feelings could land without being rushed away.

I used to wonder if the small moments really mattered once childhood passed.

Now I see how often adults return to them mentally.

How they show up in memory—not as events, but as feelings.

Family time teaches children what closeness feels like when nothing is demanded.

That lesson stays.

It shapes how they handle conflict.

How they listen.

How they remain present when relationships become complicated.

I think that's why the earlier moments don't disappear.

They become the groundwork.

The part you don't see, but rely on.

There's a comfort in knowing that family time doesn't expire.

It doesn't stop working once children grow.

It continues quietly, shaping how they relate long after the routines have changed.

I wish more parents knew this.

That the time they're investing now isn't fragile.

It's durable.

Even if childhood feels like it's slipping away, what you've built doesn't slip with it.

It stays.

In ways you won't always witness.

In moments you won't always be present for.

Family time becomes something children carry forward.

Something they draw from.

Something they recognize when they find it again in their own lives.

That's the part we don't get to see clearly.

The long arc.

The quiet influence.

When childhood moves on, family time doesn't vanish.

It becomes internal.

It turns into a sense of belonging that travels with them.

I think that's one of the most hopeful truths in parenting.

That nothing done with care is wasted.

The moments you sat together.

The conversations you didn't rush.

The presence you offered without conditions.

Those things stay.

They don't stay as memories you can revisit.

They stay as confidence.

As steadiness.

As the ability to return to connection without fear.

Childhood moves on.

But what it leaves behind is stronger than we realize.

In the final chapter, we'll talk about what it means to recognize this while there's still time—and how awareness, not urgency, is what truly changes how we show up.

16

If You're Here, You Still Have Time

There's a quiet urgency that follows many parents.

Not the loud kind.

Not panic.

Just a steady awareness that time is moving, whether we acknowledge it or not.

I used to think urgency was the enemy.

That feeling pressed to act meant something was wrong.

What I understand now is that urgency isn't always about fear.

Sometimes it's about clarity.

If you're here, reading this, it means something has already shifted.

Not in your schedule.

Not in your responsibilities.

In how you're seeing.

Time doesn't suddenly appear when we notice it.

But our relationship to it changes.

I used to think having time meant having fewer demands.

Now I know it often means having better awareness.

You don't need to reclaim childhood.

You don't need to recreate the past.

You don't need to do more.

You need to recognize what's still happening.

There's a belief that once you've missed something, it's gone forever.

That family time is a narrow window that closes completely.

That belief creates panic where none is needed.

Family time isn't a single door.

It's a series of openings.

Some wide.

Some brief.

Some quiet.

If you're here, some of those openings are still appearing.

They may look different than they used to.

They may arrive without warning.

They may not linger.

But they're there.

What matters most isn't how much time we have.

It's how we notice the time that's already unfolding.

Parents often tell themselves they'll be more present later.

When life calms down.

When things are easier.

When they feel more ready.

But presence doesn't wait for readiness.

It shows up in ordinary moments.

You don't need to rush.

Urgency doesn't mean haste.

It means attentiveness.

There's a difference between running out of time and waking

up to it.

One creates panic.

The other creates care.

If you're here, you haven't arrived too late.

You've arrived at awareness.

And awareness changes how moments land.

I've noticed that once you start seeing family time differently, it becomes harder to dismiss.

You notice the pause before a conversation ends.

You notice the invitation hidden in a casual comment.

You notice when staying a little longer matters.

Not because you're trying harder.

Because you're seeing more clearly.

This book isn't asking you to add anything to your life.

It's asking you to stop overlooking what's already there.

There will still be busy days.

There will still be missed moments.

That's not failure.

That's life.

What changes is the way you return.

The way you stay when you can.

The way you listen when it matters.

Family time doesn't demand perfection.

It responds to presence.

If there's one thing I hope stays with you, it's this:

You don't need to catch every moment.

You just need to catch some of them while they're still happening.

Those moments don't ask for grand gestures.

They ask for attention.

If you're here, you still have time.

Time to notice.

Time to stay.

Time to respond differently than you once did.

And that's enough.

Family time doesn't need to be saved.

It needs to be seen.

You're already closer than you think.

If you ever come back to these pages, it doesn't have to be because you're worried or unsure.

It can be because you want to remember what you already know.

That family time isn't something you missed or need to recover.

It's something that keeps unfolding, quietly, alongside you.

And you're already part of it.

If this book has done anything, I hope it has helped you see your own life with a little more kindness. Not as something to fix or optimize, but as something already carrying meaning. You don't need to finish this book feeling resolved. You can set it down and return to it later, the way family time itself works— quietly, without urgency. Nothing here requires you to become someone else. It only asks you to notice what you're already offering. And that is enough.

Before You Close the Book

Nothing changed today.

The house is still the same.
   The noise, the quiet, the passing through.
   A door opened and closed.
   Someone lingered.
   Someone didn't say what they almost did.
   Time kept moving,
   the way it always does—
   without asking for permission.
   And still, something was held.
   Not because it was named.
   Not because it was saved.
   Just because you were there,
   long enough
   to notice.

Author's Note

I didn't start writing this book because I had answers.

I started because I kept noticing moments I hadn't noticed before. Or maybe I noticed them too late. It's hard to tell the difference sometimes.

Like many parents, I thought I understood what mattered. I paid attention to milestones, progress, outcomes. I worried about doing things right. I worried about providing enough, guiding enough, being enough.

What I didn't understand for a long time was how quietly the most important parts were happening.

They weren't happening during big conversations or planned activities. They were happening in between. In pauses. In moments that felt too small to deserve attention.

I wrote this book as a parent who lived inside those moments without realizing what they were at the time. Not as someone looking back with certainty, but as someone looking back with clarity that arrived slowly.

There are things I wish I had understood earlier. And there are things I only understand now because time passed and changed the shape of our days.

This book isn't meant to tell you what to do.

It isn't meant to make you feel behind.

And it certainly isn't meant to add pressure to a life that already carries enough.

It's meant to sit beside you.

To name things you may have felt but never put words to. To offer recognition where advice usually shows up. To slow the moment just enough for you to see what's already there.

If some of these pages stirred something in you, that wasn't an accident. Parenting has a way of storing feelings quietly, waiting for the right moment to surface. Sometimes all it takes is seeing your own experience reflected back to you.

I don't believe there's one right way to be present.

Families are different. Children are different. Lives are different.

What matters isn't perfection.

It's attention.

And attention doesn't require a complete overhaul of your life.

It requires noticing.

Noticing when a child lingers.

Noticing when a conversation almost happens.

Noticing when silence feels settled instead of distant.

Those moments don't ask for much.

They just ask to be seen.

If you finished this book and felt a little softer toward yourself, I'm glad.

If you felt more aware—even briefly—that matters too.

Awareness doesn't demand action.

It changes how moments land.

And if you closed this book and found yourself staying just a little longer in a moment you might have rushed before, that's enough.

That's the work.

Thank you for reading slowly.

Thank you for caring deeply.

And thank you for the quiet, unseen ways you show up every day.

You're closer than you think.

About the Author

Jasvir Singh is a parent of two children and a writer who reflects on family life, time, and the quiet moments that shape relationships. His perspective comes not from theory or instruction, but from years of observing how connection forms in ordinary days—through shared silence, small conversations, and the routines families move through without noticing their weight.

He is also the author of *Raising Confident Students*, a book rooted in lived experience that explores how confidence and communication grow when children feel heard and supported. As a parent navigating academically demanding environments, Jasvir has seen firsthand how emotional steadiness, presence, and trust matter as much as achievement.

Through his writing, Jasvir speaks to busy parents who care deeply but often wonder if they are doing enough. His work offers recognition rather than advice, helping families slow down just enough to see the value of the time they are already sharing.

Also by Jasvir Singh

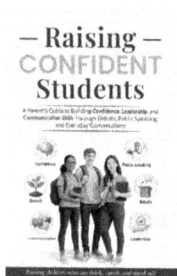

Raising Confident Students

A Parent's Guide to Building Confidence, Leadership, and Communication Skills Through Debate, Public Speaking, and Everyday Conversations

Raising Confident Students explores how confidence, communication, and leadership develop in children—not as fixed traits, but as skills shaped through everyday interactions. Drawing from real parenting experience and principles rooted in debate, public speaking, and structured conversation, the book examines why many capable children hesitate to speak and how fear of judgment takes hold.

Rather than emphasizing performance or pressure, the book focuses on listening, respectful dialogue, and low-stakes opportunities for children to think aloud, handle disagreement calmly, and advocate for themselves with clarity. Written for parents and caregivers, it offers a thoughtful, realistic approach to helping children develop a steady, resilient voice at home, at school, and beyond.